Original title:
In the Shade of Growth

Copyright © 2025 Creative Arts Management OÜ
All rights reserved.

Author: Julian Carmichael
ISBN HARDBACK: 978-1-80581-912-7
ISBN PAPERBACK: 978-1-80581-439-9
ISBN EBOOK: 978-1-80581-912-7

Rhapsody of the Resilient

In the garden, weeds wore crowns,
Dancing queens in tattered gowns.
Bugs held parties on the leaves,
Joking 'bout the nights they weave.

A flower tripped and made a scene,
Said, "Who knew dirt could be so green?"
The sunbeams laughed, a golden jest,
While bees debated who was best.

The Hidden Nest of Growth

Beneath the fern, a squirrel pranks,
Sowing acorns, giving thanks.
The roots below, they chuckle low,
As sprouts above put on a show.

A garden gnome, with painted grin,
Keeps secrets of where plants have been.
Each bud's a tale of silly strife,
From mud pies made to garden life.

Heartbeat of the Harmonious Haven

In this place where laughter's found,
Worms recite their jokes profound.
The daisies roll their yellow eyes,
As butterflies plot wild surprise.

A ladybug, dressed with flair,
Tips her spots with elegant air.
"The world is mine!" she sings with glee,
"I'll never fit in a cup of tea!"

Grace Notes in the Garden

The tulips waltz in breezy swing,
While busy ants strive to take wing.
A raindrop laughs, it's having fun,
"As I drop down, I make a pun!"

In twilight's glow, a cricket plays,
A symphony of happy days.
With each note sung, the stars applaud,
While fireflies dance on grass, quite flawed.

Lullabies of the Growing Glade

Beneath the leaves with silly glee,
The critters dance, a raucous spree.
The squirrels joke, the owls hoot loud,
While trees stand tall, forever proud.

A rabbit hops in stylish shoes,
He tells the fox, "I've got the moves!"
The brook chuckles, a watery friend,
As laughter flows and never ends.

Under the Arch of Life

In the arch where shadows play,
A snail races to win the day.
But with a wink and a dash so sly,
He trips on moss, oh me, oh my!

The butterflies giggle, twirls in flight,
While ants parade, all dressed up tight.
A beetle yells, "I'll take the lead!"
But trips on leaves, can't catch his speed!

Serene Sanctuary of the Saplings

In the grove where young ones sprout,
A tiny tree tries to shout.
"I'm the biggest!" he claims with pride,
But bends a bit, and finds he's shy!

The weeds break out in giggles loud,
As grasses sway in leafy crowd.
A worm joins in the singing fun,
Says, "I'm under you, but I've won!"

In the Embrace of the Greenery

Among the ferns, a frog in tune,
Croaks silly songs beneath the moon.
He dreams of flies in a fancy dress,
But croaks so hard, he makes a mess!

A lizard teases with bright attire,
Says, "I'll win hearts, do you require?"
But slips on dew, in quite a show,
And lands in flowers—oh what a blow!

Canopy of Continuous Change

Beneath the branches, squirrels dance,
Chasing dreams in a nut-filled trance.
Leaves giggle as they tumble down,
Twisting like a jester's crown.

Frogs in bow ties croak a tune,
While shadows waltz beneath the moon.
The breeze whispers secrets, quite absurd,
As trees laugh softly, they've heard the word.

Nurtured Under the Sky

Sunflowers wear shades, looking so cool,
Waving their heads, oh, what a school!
Bumbling bees doing pirouettes,
Gossiping flowers, no regrets!

Pants-wearing worms in a fashion parade,
Strutting their stuff in a muddy glade.
The daisies gossip, "Who wore it best?"
As the daisies bob, they are truly blessed.

Serenity in the Swelling Soil

The earth chuckles as it starts to swell,
With roots telling stories, oh so well.
Plants in pajamas, stretching wide,
Finding their rhythm, they dance with pride.

Mice in tuxedos throw a grand ball,
As the flower pots cheer, standing tall.
Worms compose music with tunes they compose,
Nature's giggles, their charm overflows.

Enchanted by the Leafy Light

Nature's chandeliers swing and sway,
As sunlight plays in a devil-may-care way.
Chickens wear crowns, clucking with style,
While rabbits hop in a dapper aisle.

The breeze brings whispers, a thrilling tease,
As crickets hold meetings beneath the trees.
With mushrooms in hats, they toast with glee,
To the quaint moments, forever carefree.

The Understory of Ambition

In the jungle of dreams, a snail races,
Laughing at turtles with smug little faces.
Ambition can climb, but don't trip on roots,
When the grass is too tall, mind the sneaky boots.

Frogs croak their wisdom from lily pad thrones,
While rabbits plot paths to steal all your cones.
Chasing the sun, they all end up stuck,
In a field full of weeds, just plain rotten luck.

Vitality in the Shade of Time

Life's like a fruit that's ripening slow,
But watch out for worms that wiggle below.
In the rustling leaves, you might find a joke,
As squirrels debate the best nut to poke.

With laughter like raindrops that dance on the ground,
And dreams that grow taller, but never quite sound.
Time stretches, it bends, and it sometimes forgets,
Like the cat who's convinced it pays off its debts.

Beneath the Arching Boughs

Under trees that gossip, we plot our schemes,
While the squirrels mock us, nothing's as it seems.
Leaves tap their feet to a quirky old tune,
As the sun throws confetti, the world gets a boon.

We gather our dreams in a silly parade,
With daisies and dandelions having a spade.
Together we chuckle at mischief we make,
Like planting our hopes in a cupcake-shaped lake.

Horizon of Nurtured Aspirations

In fields of desire, we plant all our wishes,
Frolicking creatures swap tales and some dishes.
With each passing cloud that drifts overhead,
We grow roots in the fun, while nobody's fed.

As bees buzz around with their quirky dance moves,
We question the wisdom of grown-up approved grooves.
In this garden of giggles, who needs the grind?
We'll sprout joy and laughter; it's wealth that we find.

Haven of Hopeful Harbors

In a harbor bright and cheery,
Docked a boat quite big and leery.
Its captain lost his map and plans,
Sailing on, with ducks as fans.

Seagulls laugh, a squawking cheer,
The crew just hands them bits of beer.
Yet hope remains on every shore,
As waves keep coming, wanting more.

Underneath the Angelic Arbour

Beneath a tree with branches wide,
Squirrels play their acorn slide.
They gather nuts, their secret stash,
Then giggle as they make a splash.

A butterfly in pink and blue,
Spies the antics and joins too.
In laughter shared, they lose their fears,
And dance until the autumn nears.

Sunshine's Dance with the Shadows

Sunshine winks at shadows shy,
They twirl and spin, oh my, oh my!
A flicker here, a prankster there,
They play tag without a care.

The daisies chuckle at the game,
Bowing down to their best fame.
With every flip and gleeful sway,
They light the world in sudden play.

The Progress of the Peeking Buds

Little buds peek out with glee,
Stretching limbs like they're a spree.
A nearby flower starts to pout,
'Hey, what's this fuss? Get out, get out!'

But buds just giggle, bloom a bit,
With colors bright, they choose to flit.
Their petals dance, a cheeky spree,
The garden laughs, as happy as can be.

Shadows of Aspiration

Under the tree, a dream takes flight,
Squirrels debating who owns the height.
Branches are arms, waving 'hello',
While chatting leaves steal the show!

A small acorn whispered, 'I'm a star!',
Next to it, a mushroom said, 'Not so far!'.
With every gust, laughter is tossed,
In this world, all worries are lost!

The roots chuckle deep as they connect,
While the sunbeams dance, all smiles perfect.
Each flower prances, a colorful sight,
In this grove, even shadows feel light!

Roots of Resilience

Wiggly roots with stories to tell,
They anchor dreams, oh so well.
Through storms and winds, they gently sway,
Making a big fuss about the day!

Beneath the soil, they tickle and tease,
While worms play tag with wriggly ease.
'Throw me a challenge!' one root did shout,
The others laughed, 'Just chill out!'

They stretch and groan, but laugh out loud,
At the silly humans lost in the crowd.
These tough old roots know how to play,
Resilience thrives in a funny way!

A Sanctuary of Green

In a cozy nook where giggles bloom,
Laughter echoes within nature's room.
Bumblebees buzz, wearing tiny hats,
While grass blades wiggle, making chats!

Sunflowers sway, in matching boots,
Dancing around like late-night hoots.
'Watch my splits!' one daisy did boast,
While others turned pale, lacking the toast!

The breeze pulls faces, tickles the leaves,
A place of wonder, oh how it believes!
In this sanctuary, joy takes a stand,
With greens that giggle across the land!

The Pulse of Progress

Bees with briefcases buzzing by fast,
Chasing dreams that never quite last.
Each petal pushing a hearty request,
To bloom and shine, to be their best!

A ladybug claimed, 'I'm the next big hit!',
While ants formed a band, not ready to quit.
With soil as their stage, the fun starts bright,
Even the slugs sing, under soft twilight!

Roots are the heartbeat, pumping with glee,
Every sprout a new opportunity!
With humor and hope, they rise and move,
This rhythm of life is such a groove!

The Gentle Rise of Green Dreams

A tiny seed once took a nap,
It dreamed of leaves and quite a gap.
The neighbors chuckled, 'What a joke!'
Yet out it sprouted, a leafy bloke.

It wobbled high and swayed with glee,
While bugs held parties, wild and free.
'I'm not just grass!' it shouted loud,
As worms lined up, all very proud.

Tall sunflowers snickered, 'Look at that!'
But little sprout wore a spiffy hat.
With daisies dancing, all in a line,
They laughed and sang, a joyful sign.

So here's to dreams that rise with cheer,
Bringing craziness and good old beer!
For in this garden, bright and bright,
Funny things grow out of sight!

Symphony of Subtle Growth.

With gentle whispers, sprouts did play,
They held a concert not far away.
A penguin tap danced on the green,
With bugs as musicians, quite the scene!

The daisies clapped in rhythm divine,
While grasshoppers strummed on their twine.
'What a treat!' the garden cheered,
As frogs croaked loudly, no one steered.

A shy old tree hummed the tune,
While roots jiggled beneath the moon.
Leaves laughed out loud, swirling 'round,
In this leafy bash, joy abounds!

So if you see a garden pot,
Remember the laughter, it's quite a lot!
Growth brings giggles, and that's not tough,
For life's a dance with just enough fluff!

Whispers of the Flourishing

Among the petals, a sweet surprise,
The daisies giggled, oh such lies!
A snail wore shades, quite out of place,
As ladybirds formed a tiny race.

Chasing dreams, they'd shuffle about,
While pumpkin vines went on a pout.
'Why won't they notice my fancy flair?'
They waved at bees buzzing in the air.

A tall green stalk with arms so long,
Would tickle blades to join the song.
'Who knew we'd thrive and steal the bliss?'
They danced and twirled like nothing amiss.

In this riot of colors and play,
The garden chuckles, brightens the day.
So spot the quirks, embrace the fun,
For when growth whispers, mischief's begun!

Shadows of the Canopy

Under leafy roofs, the shadows laugh,
As plants tell tales on their leafy path.
A ceiling of green, what a wild sight,
While squirrels debate if acorns are right.

The ferns flip-flop, dancing in shade,
While crooked branches hum the parade.
Rabbits hop in with a shimmy and sway,
Competing for carrots, they munched all day.

Beneath the tall oaks, a racket ensued,
As critters held meetings, plotting or crude.
'A leaf fell down, what a catastrophe!'
Yet giggles erupted, 'Just let it be!'

In this cozy nook where whispers fly,
Silly shadows make the hours spry.
So laugh along with nature's jest,
For in leafy lanes, we're truly blessed!

The Stillness of Rising

In the garden, squirrels dance,
Chasing shadows, taking a chance.
A tomato plant wears a frown,
While beans climb slowly, looking down.

Sunflowers giggle at the ants,
Who march in lines, donning tiny pants.
The cucumbers roll, feeling bold,
Whispering secrets, their tales unfold.

A butterfly sneezes in bright delight,
Stirring the daisies, oh what a sight!
While lettuce plays hide and seek,
Laughing at rabbits, it's quite the peek.

The sun winks down with a radiant grin,
As the herbs concoct a plan to win.
In this silly patch, joy is rife,
Nature's laughter fuels this life.

Sheltered by Nature's Grace

Rabbits munch grass in a sprightly race,
With cabbage hearts, they've found their place.
A wise old oak, chuckling away,
Says, "Lettuce be friends, let's play!"

Butterflies wear polka dot coats,
And gossip like birds, sharing their notes.
A friendly gopher digs with flair,
Whistling tunes from his underground lair.

The flowers nod in hues so bright,
Finding humor in the morning light.
Petunias blush, the daisies cheer,
Upon their petals, joy is clear.

The breeze carries laughter 'neath the sun,
As nature plays games that never shun.
In this haven of green, all is well,
With giggles and whispers, who can't tell?

Veiled Growth in Quiet Corners

In corners hidden, peas do sway,
Winking at friends in a playful display.
Mice hold a meeting under a leaf,
They plot mischief and munch on beef!

The sweet corn stands tall, feeling grand,
Sharing tall tales of the great garden land.
While radishes blush deep crimson red,
Wishing they'd change what they'd said.

The carrots chuckle beneath the earth,
Reminiscing on their humble birth.
As shadows stretch from plants on high,
Sunbeams bounce, the laughter won't die.

Bamboo giggles, swaying in glee,
With roots all tickled, oh can't you see?
In this cloak of green, a jest unfolds,
Nature's a prankster, let the fun be told.

The Lush Corridor of Promise

Down the path, where peppers pose,
Winking at onions, striking a prose.
A hedgehog spins tales of yore,
While thyme writes sonnets on the floor.

The giddy chard, with colors so bright,
Pulls pranks on squash all day and night.
With giggles hidden in the breeze,
Complaining broccoli catches a freeze!

Pumpkins roll, telling jokes in the sun,
While zucchinis laugh, saying, "We're all one!"
The berries gossip, painting the air,
With stories of sugar and creamy fare.

As bees buzz softly in a line,
They share their secrets, "Is that a sign?"
In this lush world, joy sprouts and blooms,
Echoing laughter in nature's rooms.

Sowing Seeds of Serenity

I tossed some seeds into the air,
Hoping for a garden without a care.
But daisies sprouted with hats so wide,
I swear they giggled as they tried to hide.

The carrots wore socks, what a silly sight,
Beneath their tops, they danced with delight.
While turtles spun tales of their high-speed race,
Flipping over flowers, oh, what a place!

Treetops and Dreams

Up in the branches, birds play charades,
While squirrels discuss, in the sun's warm glades.
The wise old owl rolls his eyes in the breeze,
As the chipmunks complain, 'The acorns aren't peas!'

Leaves whisper secrets with a ticklish cheer,
While ants hold a meeting, their boss can't hear.
Yet laughter resounds from a frog on a swing,
A true maestro of this woodland bling!

Beneath the Burgeoning Branches

Beneath the canopy, shadows play tricks,
Where mushrooms wear helmets, and clovers do flips.
A wisecracking lizard declared it a day,
While worms rolled in laughter, their backs on display.

Dandelions giggle as the breezes blow,
'We're fluffier now, thanks to the show!'
A dancing grasshopper lost in a groove,
Challenges a beetle to show off a move!

The Harmony of Hidden Growth

In a patch of green, a curious sprout,
Said, 'I can sing! But there's a twist, no doubt.'
A rabbit retorted, 'That's quite a tall tale,
But I'll hum along if you don't go pale!'

With frogs as the chorus and ants in the band,
The beetles tap dance on the flower bed stand.
Oh, what a concert beneath the bright sky,
Even the clouds giggle as they drift by!

Cradled by the Earth's Whisper

Beneath the soil, worms do dance,
While daisies giggle in a trance.
The acorn ponders, with a grin,
'If squirrels steal me, where to begin?'

Raindrops drum a silly tune,
While daisies fashion hats by noon.
A sprout sneezes, 'Excuse me, please!'
As butterflies dance on the breeze.

The sun pulls a face, bright and round,
While plants imitate, swaying profound.
A garden party—who wants cake?
The veggies laugh, but some might quake!

With roots entwined, they plot their fun,
Sipping dew like it's a pun.
Beneath the green, the laughter's deep,
As nature whispers, 'Time for sleep!'

Sowing Seeds of Tomorrow

Tiny seeds with dreams so grand,
Plotting futures just as planned.
They wiggle, giggle, and take flight,
In the dark, they outsmart the night.

The gardener trips, oh what a show,
His shovel's dancing—very slow.
Seeds shout, 'Look, we've got a fan!'
While patchy weeds form a band.

They plot to grow in funny shapes,
An onion in a cloak escapes.
Tomatoes roll, thinking they're stars,
As carrots joke about their scars.

Watering can spills its dreams,
As laughter bursts in sunny beams.
In a world where veggies beam,
They giggle on, in moonlight's gleam.

When Leaves Speak of Hope

Whispers flutter in leaf attire,
'Watch us grow, we're never tired!'
A dandelion makes a wish,
'Just one more chance, I'll be delicious!'

The oak tree chuckles at the breeze,
'Take a break, you're not a tease!'
'I'm just a twig with grand ambitions,'
Replies a young sprout with wild visions.

In the forest, mischief's alive,
With pinecones plotting, 'Let's all thrive!'
They roll and tumble, almost right,
'Is that a tree? No, what a sight!'

As shadows stretch and laughter swells,
Even the crickets hear the bells.
Leaves rustle secrets in the night,
Dreaming of futures shining bright.

Canopy of Gentle Dreams

Underneath the leafy dome,
Frogs hope for a splashy home.
While ants parade in tiny hats,
The fireflies buzz, 'We're acrobats!'

Beneath the branches, shadows play,
With sunbeams teasing throughout the day.
The mushrooms giggle, round and spry,
'We're the pillows where dreams can fly!'

A sloth remarks with a lazy grin,
'Why rush it, when you can spin?'
As butterflies twirl in the light,
Nature giggles, everything's right.

With each breeze, the world's a jest,
As animals frolic, feeling blessed.
In this canopy, joy takes flight,
Beneath the stars, hearts feel light.

Sprouts of Embrace

Tiny shoots in pots, they dance,
Reaching high, they take their chance.
They say, 'Hey sun, throw us light!'
While roots hold tight, they giggle with delight.

Worms wiggle close, they start to tease,
'Why don't you grow a little more, please?'
Each leaf a laugh, each stem a cheer,
In the garden, there's nothing to fear.

A squirrel snickers, 'Look at those greens!'
Dancing like they're on movie screens.
Pollen party, all buzzing around,
Nature's own version of merry-go-round.

So here's to sprouts with flair and might,
Growing tall with silly heights.
They dream of heights, of wide, blue skies,
With roots too stubborn to say goodbyes!

Growth's Gentle Camouflage

Petunias dressed in purple frocks,
Hiding marigolds in silly socks.
Stems do a jig, leaves play peek-a-boo,
A grand masquerade, in morning dew.

A garden where veggies share the stage,
Tomatoes wink, oh what a rage!
Cabbage rolls, with leaves in a curl,
'Watch us grow, we're quite the swirl!'

In this patch, we joke and play,
'Grow a little faster, hip-hip-hooray!'
Pumpkins chuckle, kicking up dirt,
While carrots blush in their orange shirt.

So here's to growth, that sly disguise,
Where laughter sprouts and friendship lies.
A secret club of leafy mates,
Blooming fun, writing garden fates.

Tapestry of Emerging Lives

From tiny seeds to a patchwork bloom,
Sprinkled laughter fills the room.
Potatoes rolling, 'We're set to fry!'
While onions giggle, asking, 'Oh, my?'

A sunflower shows off its sunny face,
Dancing 'round like it owns the place.
Bees buzzing past with sticky feet,
'Bring on the nectar, it can't be beat!'

Peppers prance in colors bright,
'Come join the fun, it's a hoot tonight!'
In this tapestry, we joke and tease,
Joining hands, just to please.

An oak tree chuckles, long and wise,
Watching sprouts under happy skies.
Together we grow, in a jolly dance,
Every life here takes a chance.

Secret Gardens of Potential

Behind the fence, where gnomes stand watch,
Lies a garden of dreams, it's quite the catch.
Here, beans make wishes, climbing up high,
While garlic grumbles, 'Why pass me by?'

Radishes whisper, 'You've got to dig!'
Beneath the surface, we're all quite big.
Zucchinis love dress-ups, strutting in style,
While peas play tag, going the extra mile.

Between the blooms, laughter weaves tight,
Little buds grinning with pure delight.
In this secret world, potential swells,
With every giggle, life gently tells.

So let's tiptoe in, partake in the fun,
Together we shine, like the morning sun.
In these hidden patches, dreams twirl and spin,
A secret garden, where we all begin.

Journey Through the Firmament

I tripped on a cloud, oh what a ride,
The stars all giggled, as they tried to hide.
A comet zoomed past with a wink and a wave,
Said, "Chasing your dreams? Be brave, be brave!"

Fell headfirst into a nebula stew,
Thought it was soup, but it's just chilly goo.
Aliens laughed, with their green, silly hats,
"Join us for a dance, and forget the spats!"

So floated along, with a heart full of fun,
In the cosmic circus, oh, wasn't it run!
I ended the trip with a saucer of pie,
And a starfish said, "Hey! Want to give it a try?"

Back on Earth, with a smile on my face,
I'd trade it for nothing, that wild, wacky space!

The Pull of the Rooted

Down in the dirt, the roots start to play,
"Hey, can you tickle?" I heard one say.
They wiggled and jiggled, all covered in mud,
I laughed at the sight, a most jolly thud!

"Gravity's a hoot!" the carrot did cheer,
"Pull us down deeper, we'll grow without fear!"
The potatoes were chuckling, playing it cool,
"Join us for a game? We've built a deep pool!"

So I dove right in, with plants all around,
Splashing and laughing, what joy I found!
But then came the rain, and what a wide scene,
We floated like champions—root veggies supreme!

From mud to the sky, what a marvelous trip,
Echoes of laughter from every green lip!

Guardian of the Grassy Grove

In the grove where the grass does a jig and a twirl,
Lives a gopher named Gary, who's quite the squirrel.
With teeth like a comb and a hat made of leaves,
He patrols the green realm, while the critters all weave.

"Watch out for the foxes!" Gary chimes loud,
While bees throw a bash, oh what a crowd!
He sets up the snacks, with acorns and jam,
A disco party—oh yeah, that's the plan!

The butterflies twirl, wearing glittery wings,
While Gary hums tunes, and the meadowbird sings.
With every good dance, and every mad jest,
Life in the grove is surely the best!

From dusk until dawn, let the laughter run free,
In Gary's green kingdom, come play with me!

Whispering Leaves of Learning

In the student treehouse, all branches aflutter,
Leaves whisper secrets, like moms with a shudder.
"Did you hear the news?" a young twig did squeak,
"The oak's been found snoozing, haven't heard a peak!"

Then old Maple laughed, with a crack in her bark,
"Let's prank the acorns, give them a spark!"
They threw paper planes, made of colorful hues,
Oh the giggles that followed, the laughter ensues!

The clouds rolled in, for a school-day surprise,
Rain turned to laughter, oh my, what a prize!
With drips and with drops, they danced in the rain,
Learning's all fun when you laugh through the pain!

So if you feel lost, just look to the trees,
Whispered wisdom is carried in the breeze!

Echoes of the Nurtured Roots

Beneath the earth, a party swells,
The worms dance round, and soil compels.
"Dig here!" they cheer, with bites of cheer,
As seedlings giggle, drawing near.

The carrots gossip, the radishes jest,
All in a ruckus, they're feeling blessed.
"Who knew being buried could be so fine?
Let's root for each other, and all will shine!"

A radish dressed in leafy flair,
Claims to be the veggie queen with flair.
"Watch out, folks, I'm quite the catch!
With a dip of ranch, I'm truly a match!"

And while above, a bird will sing,
The veggies chuckle, doing their thing.
With every sprout, they share a laugh,
"Growing's the fun part, do the worm dance and laugh!"

Embrace of the Flourishing Foliage

Leaves in the breeze, a jolly crew,
They sway and twist, as if they knew.
"Let's have a contest of who's got the flair,
With flips and spins, we'll dance in the air!"

A sunflower yawns, waking from sleep,
"It's time to grow tall, no time for a creep!"
With petals bright like a vibrant cape,
"I'll outshine the clouds and escape the drape!"

The ivy claims it's the fastest to climb,
While the daisies giggle and snack on thyme.
"Hey, leafy friends, let's not be coy,
Life's a wild ride; it's all pure joy!"

So under the sun, they shimmer and glide,
The flora befriends, no need to hide.
Together they thrive, with laughter a-peal,
In this green carnival, it's all about zeal!

The Refuge of Feathered Leaves

Branches up high, where birds take a seat,
"Tweet my song, it's a champion beat!"
With feathers afluff, they hold a grand show,
"Did you hear the one about the bug in tow?"

A squirrel looks on, munching on snacks,
"With you all up there, I'll stick to my tracks.
'Cause if I climb, when you jokes fly,
I might just miss, and land in a pie!"

So they flit and dive, like acrobats bold,
With tales of adventures, never grow old.
"Just one more joke, then we'll take a rest,
You know we're the best; it's simply a jest!"

As dusk rolls in, they wrap up their night,
With a wink and a nod, they bid each a flight.
Laughter echoes in those leafy domains,
A refuge of joy, free from all chains!

Cradled by the Emerging Green

In a patch of sun, the seedlings play,
"Who can stretch the furthest, come what may?"
The broccoli boasts, "I'm bound for the sky!"
While peas shout out, "We'll give it a try!"

"Don't forget us!" the onions call,
"While you all reach, we're ready to sprawl!"
With ties of the earth, and fun of the sun,
Each sprout is a champion, on the run!

As ladybugs giggle, they hitch a ride,
Along the green stalks, with nothing to hide.
"Let's race in the breeze, it's a splendid day,
No ifs or buts, we're here to play!"

And so they grow, in laughter entwined,
In a world of whimsy, they are combined.
With roots in the ground and hearts taking flight,
They dance in the warmth, all through the night!

Hidden Blooms of Change

A flower peeked from under a rock,
It whispered loudly, "I'm quite the shock!"
The bees all laughed, a honeyed cheer,
"You've got some guts, oh look, my dear!"

In a pot by the window, a sprout took a nap,
While a cat plotted its next silly trap.
"Who knew plants dream of adventures grand?"
"I swear I saw mine playing in a band!"

The garden party was all the rage,
With veggies dancing, taking the stage.
Tomatoes twirled, in disco lights,
Cucumbers laughed at their awkward sights!

Underneath these blooms so bold and bright,
There are secrets hiding, what a delight!
Each petal tickling the softest breeze,
Plant antics fill the air with such ease!

Underneath the Verdant Veil

Beneath green layers, mischief awaits,
A snail's a dancer, twisting on plates.
"Look at me glide!" it laughed with glee,
"I'm faster than you!" (pretending, you see!)

The ferns were gossiping, tea in their cups,
"Did you hear the news? A raccoon drums up!"
They chuckled and rustled, a leafy spree,
Sipping dew drops, as jolly as can be!

A pebble turned prince, with a crown made of moss,
Declared a kingdom, and not at a loss.
"All who dare knock, please, wipe your feet!"
And the earthworms danced, tapping to the beat!

With twinkling eyes, the blossoms recount,
Adventures of squirrels that bravely surmount.
In this verdant world, laughter shall reign,
Every green corner has joy to gain!

Echoes of Flourishing Silence

In the hushed corners, a plot brewed deep,
The daisies conspired while others would sleep.
"What if we splash some paint in the night?"
"Or wear funny hats? Oh, what a sight!"

A bold little seed went sprouting with flair,
"Watch me take flight, oh do if you dare!"
But the wind replied with a gentle whoosh,
"You'll need a helmet before you go push!"

Amid buzzing laughter and rustling leaves,
A worm set up shop, selling pretend weaves.
"For silk of the spider, I'll trade you some dirt!"
Said the ladybug, "Just don't squish my skirt!"

In echoes of stillness, fun high above,
Nature's a playground, with all kinds of love.
Every giggle and chuckle, trees sway and bend,
Listen closely, dear friend, this joy will not end!

The Hushed Strength of Saplings

Little saplings giggle, trying to stand,
Huddled together, forming a band.
They'd sway in the breeze, singing their tune,
"If we hit the right notes, we might be a boon!"

With roots tangled tight, they plotted a scene,
"Let's have a party, it'll be quite keen!"
The mushrooms agreed, wearing hats made of clay,
While the twigs played the banjo, hip hip hooray!

On a foggy morn, they gathered around,
To chant silly songs without a sound.
Their leaves danced lively, in shades of bright hue,
"Who knew being quiet could feel so new?"

So under the boughs where laughter's unfurled,
The saplings remind us: it's a playful world.
In whispers and giggles, their strength is revealed,
Together in silence, they joyously appealed!

Cradle of the Climbing Vines

A vine who dreamed to reach the sky,
But paused to sip on dew nearby.
"Why climb so high?" the daisies asked,
"When there's a snack right here, unmasked!"

The climbing tendrils start to sway,
As squirrels dance, making their play.
With each twist, they say with glee,
"Let's make this trellis a climbing spree!"

A ladybug hops up to chat,
"This vine's going nowhere—what of that?"
But the vine just laughs, sways to and fro,
"I'm staying grounded; come join the show!"

In laughter, they all intertwine,
A party planned in leaves, divine.
For vines or flowers, who needs a lift?
When joy is found right here—a gift!

Conversations with the Clusters

A cluster of grapes, so round and bright,
Gossiping under the soft moonlight.
"Did you hear the peach's latest scheme?"
"She's planning to be the star of the cream!"

They giggle and bounce, in sweet delight,
While bees buzz around, taking flight.
"What about the melons?" one grape chimes,
"They've got the juiciest gossip this time!"

With a raucous laugh, they share their tales,
Of radishes lost and runaway snails.
"Life's too short for hanging tight,"
Said the clusters as the stars shone bright!

One sweet grape slid down with a clatter,
"Who needs fancy? All that's what matters!"
They rolled around, letting laughter flow,
In joyful chaos, their seeds did sow!

The Pathway of Petal and Stem

With petals fluttering, a dance so grand,
Two roses emerged, hand in hand.
"Shall we stroll down this leafy lane?"
"Oh, let's see whose thorns bring the pain!"

Their vibrant colors gleamed in the light,
Arguing softly, but all in delight.
"I'm more fragrant!" one rose proclaimed,
"But I've got the charm!" the other claimamed.

The daisies giggled from their cozy spots,
At the playful jabs and show-off plots.
"Why not make flower crowns for fun?"
They burst into laughter; the battle was won!

With petals tangled in joy and cheer,
They danced and twirled, without any fear.
In this garden, with roots so deep,
The way of petals was a joyous leap!

Beneath the Boughs of Blessings

Under boughs where the shadows play,
A little squirrel scours his day.
"What's on the menu?" he asks with glee,
"Acorns, nuts—it's a feast, you see!"

Branches chuckle with leaves so bright,
As laughter echoes in the soft twilight.
"Why are you hoarding?" a bird did say,
"Share the bounty and join the play!"

With a wink, the squirrel made his call,
"A nutty party—come one, come all!"
Apples and berries joined in the fun,
Beneath the boughs, warmth for everyone!

They danced in circles, around the tree,
Each found a friend, wild and free.
In shadows grand where laughter sings,
The joy of life and the love it brings!

The Quiet Strength of the Stem

Beneath the soil they quietly play,
Roots tickle worms, in a subterranean ballet.
A stem stands tall with a wink of delight,
Saying, "I won't fall, though I sway in the night!"

Leaves in a flutter, gossip and tease,
"Did you see that bug? He brought me to my knees!"
With whispers of laughter, they dance in the breeze,
A green little party, oh what a tease!

Despite the storms that may come and go,
They chuckle together, saying, "We'll steal the show!"
For even in earth, there's laughter to find,
Life's a vine-coated joke, one of a kind!

So here's to the stem, so sturdy and sly,
Keeping the secrets that dance in the sky.
With roots deep in humor and tops in bright cheer,
They remind us to laugh, as the sunshine draws near.

Flourish in the Friendliness of Ferns

In the cozy corner, the ferns like to chat,
Sharing tall tales about a washed-up cat.
"Once I was just fronds, not a clue in the world,"
Said a cheeky young leaf, with her edges all curled.

Their neighbors, the daisies, tease them at night,
"Why don't you all party? You're hiding your light!"
But ferns just giggle, with a graceful bow,
"We prefer our shade; it's like a soft meow!"

Each frond's like a dancer, so swish and so swirl,
Twirling in whispers like a feathery whirl.
Together they flourish, a fussy brigade,
In the friendliness of greens, no need to parade!

So here's to the ferns, with their cheeky sense of fun,
Guardians of laughter, always on the run.
With stories aplenty and time to confide,
Life's simply more leafy when they're by your side!

Cascades of Color and Care

In gardens where colors tumble and play,
A splash of bright petals in sweet disarray.
A purple-faced pansy, with jokes up her sleeve,
"I bloom just for fun, so don't you leave!"

Marigolds giggle in fading sunset light,
Saying, "We're crisp, but we still look all right!"
With each little breeze, they twirl like a dance,
And beg the sun-drops for one more chance.

The daisies, they crown with innocent flair,
"Catch us if you can! We're too quick to care!"
They leap on the wind, round and round they spin,
Petals just fluttering, let the games begin!

In cascades of laughter, they blend and they sway,
A riot of colors, in bright disarray.
So grab a bouquet of cheer and delight,
Join the flow of the fun, from morning till night!

The Whispering Winds of Change

The winds come sneaking, with stories to tell,
Whispering secrets, it's quite a hard sell.
"Did you hear? That tree thinks it's taller than me!"
Said a breeze full of mischief, quite full of glee.

Chasing the clouds, they giggle and sway,
Fetching the leaves for a playful display.
"Let's spin in a circle! We'll dance through the town!"
The branches all trembled, then let their hair down!

As seasons change hands, with a wink and a nod,
The winds toss around, like a playful old broad.
"Time to swap colors!" they declare with a cheer,
For laughter's the wind, always coming near!

So next time it breezes, don't take it for granted,
Join in the fun, let your heart feel enchanted.
The winds know the secrets of joy and of play,
Bring your own laughter, come dance in the sway!

Harmony of Branch and Blossom

Leaves are laughing, swaying high,
Twigs gossip softly, oh my my!
Petals dance like they know a joke,
While acorns tumble, a clumsy bloke.

Squirrels giggle, chasing their tails,
Bark-covered trees, telling tales.
Insects buzz with a cheeky grin,
In this leafy party, we all win!

Fragrant blooms with a hint of sass,
Pollen party—everyone's got class.
The breeze winks, a playful tease,
Nature's humor, puts us at ease.

Roots tickle underground, who knew?
The soil sings—a laugh or two.
Sunbeams tickle the vibrant scene,
In this garden, we're all quite keen.

Collective Breath of the Grove

In the crowd, they twist and shout,
Roots holding hands, dancing about.
Breezes chuckle, rustling leaves,
A symphony of laughter weaves.

Branches swaying, full of cheer,
Mossy stone has jokes to share.
The sun's a joker, peeking through,
Painting shadows, life anew.

Flowers play hide and seek with bees,
A ticklish whiff in the gentle breeze.
Laughter echoes, nature's delight,
As flora beams in morning light.

Giggling grasses sway and bend,
Each sprout knows it's fun to pretend.
Earth chuckles with a hearty grin,
In this grove, we all fit in!

Embracing the Green Souls

With every sprout, there's giggles wide,
Ferns whisper secrets, their hearts open wide.
The daisies chuckle, sharing a wink,
While dandelions puff, love on the brink.

Branches hold up signs of cheer,
Artsy bark makes the laughter clear.
A squirrel's prank? A nutty stew,
In this wild laughter, we find our crew.

Roots play twister, tangled and tight,
They keep it lively throughout the night.
Glowworms giggle, lighting the way,
In the green embrace, we frolic and sway.

Joyful greens hum their sweet refrain,
The dance of life, a tickle of rain.
In this vibrant world, we all convene,
With smiles so wide, we're evergreen!

Shadows of Nurtured Souls

Under branches, where fun takes flight,
The shadows chat, teasing the light.
Each leaf a laugh, a joke well spun,
In the green glow, we're all just fun.

Tiny worms wiggle, share their tales,
While sunbeams peek, and everyone hails.
The grass sings low, a tickling tune,
In the theater of roots, we all swoon.

Clouds drift through, casting playful spells,
With every rustle, the heartbeat swells.
A shady nook holds delight so grand,
As we sway and giggle in this band.

Nature's laughter echoes far and wide,
In the warmth of the shade, we all abide.
With nurturing love and humor bold,
The stories of life, forever told.

Cultivating Connections Over Canopies

Under the branches, we giggle and play,
Finding lost acorns, come join the fray!
Squirrels pass secrets with twitchy little tails,
As we stomp through the leaves, like clumsy footed whales.

Friends gather round as the branches entwine,
Whispering jokes over mulberry wine.
Laughter erupts when the birds start to sing,
Making odd dance moves like they're daring spring.

We pitch a grand tent from the old weaves of fate,
Dressed like wild jesters, we're never too late.
Colliding with critters, we share silly tales,
As shadows start laughing—oh, what fun prevails!

Our picnic spreads wide on a blanket of green,
With snacks that are questionable but always seen.
Chasing each other like leaves in a breeze,
Creating our own glee, as easy as you please.

The Symphony of Roots and Rains

A tap dance of droplets on the leafy expanse,
Each puddle a stage for the worms' wiggly dance.
Roots hum a tune, in their underground plot,
While the carrots just giggle, in their cozy little spot.

The radishes rally for a concert tonight,
Promising rhythms that will surely delight.
With onions on keys and potatoes on drums,
The garden's a ruckus, oh hear how it hums!

When the rainstorm retreats and the sun takes a bow,
We huddle in corners, and swing like a cow.
The daffodils chuckle as they sway to the beat,
In this musical maze where the fun never meets.

So gather your friends, bring your dubious snacks,
Join roots in their roots as we all take some cracks.
With laughter like raindrops, falling all 'round,
We create our own symphony, joy will abound!

The Hidden Heart of the Harvest

Boots caked in mud, oh what a delight,
Finding treasures, oh, what a sight!
Carrots like sabers, shining with glee,
Tell me, is there anything sweeter than me?

Potatoes with wigs, they hide from the sun,
Peas pop out laughing, all having their fun.
Tomatoes are blushing, they're shy, don't you see?
While cucumbers giggle with glee from their spree.

We dig in the soil, unearthing some cheer,
Each turn reveals secrets, oh how we revere!
Beets are in costume, all dressed up in style,
Making us laugh, they're sure worth the while!

With baskets overflowing, the harvest is grand,
Each vegetable smile, a gift from the land.
So savor the humor that each plant will impart,
As we dance through the rows, it's a joy to take part.

Life's Melody in the Meadows

Mice in the meadow, they organize a play,
Acorns as drums; oh come join the fray!
Everyone's dancing, beneath a sunflower,
Nothing but laughter and joy fills the hour.

Bouncing like bunnies, they hop to the beat,
Swinging their ears like they're moving their feet.
Playing tag with shadows, they run and they hide,
Each tumble, each trip, is a rollercoaster ride.

The daisies lean in with a curious glance,
As the kids spin circles, lost in the dance.
With laughter that echoes, they jump and they shout,
While clouds drift above, in this sunny bout.

In meadows of giggles, the fun takes its flight,
Life flows like music, from morning till night.
So tiptoe through grasses, where joy will unfold,
And be part of a story, just waiting to be told.

The Serene Path Through the Undergrowth

Amidst the leaves, we walk with ease,
Dodging spiders like they're high-speed bees.
The rabbits watch, they giggle and hop,
As we stumble round every tree and drop.

The squirrels tease us, they throw acorns,
"Can't you find your way, amidst these thorns?"
We laugh it off, our compass is fun,
While nature giggles in the setting sun.

Frogs croak tunes that make us prance,
Each splashy leap is a silly dance.
With every step, we trip and we giggle,
As nature's jesters cause us to wiggle.

Yet in this maze, we find a plot,
Where nothing's lost and all is sought.
We stroll along, just two old goats,
And nature chuckles at our silly thought.

Nature's Quiet Nurture

Leaves whisper tales of their wild pursuits,
While ants march by in their shiny boots.
The sun peeks through with a cheeky grin,
As we try to fit in, but we just can't win.

A deer prances past, its tail in the air,
"Don't mind me, I'm just a bit more rare!"
We chuckle along with the crickets' song,
As the trees nod their heads, all day long.

With mushrooms sprouting like goofy hats,
And squirrels doing acrobatics like brats.
We slip on the moss, oh what a thrill,
As nature's humor gives us a chill.

But here we dwell, in this vibrant sprawl,
Amongst the laughter, we stand tall.
What joy it brings to wander and roam,
In nature's arms, we'll always feel home.

Beneath the Elder's Embrace

An old tree stands, with wisdom profound,
Its branches echo laughter all around.
We sit at its roots, with snacks in hand,
As shadows dance on the bright, soft sand.

The leaves above break into a laugh,
When we miscount, our simple math.
The wind joins in with playful breeze,
While critters giggle and do as they please.

With twilight's glow, the fireflies blink,
While we debate the color of ink.
"Are they blue or just yellow?" we gleefully guess,
As nature rolls over, amused by the mess.

Under this arch, we share our dreams,
With echoes reflected like sunlit beams.
In this quirky realm where giggles entwine,
We find our laughter, a drink so divine.

Tapestry of Time and Tendrils

In this woven space where the vines interlace,
We stumble upon the oddest of grace.
Grass tickles our toes, the ferns wave goodbye,
As we jokingly ponder how far we'd fly.

Bumblebees buzz with attitude bold,
While blossoms take bets on who'll be scolded.
"Don't touch that one!" our friend shouts with glee,
As we giggle and sway like the leaves of the tree.

The breeze carries whispers from branches above,
Teasing our hearts in a dance we all love.
With every twist in this vibrant maze,
We spin and we twirl, lost in the haze.

And as day fades into evening's hue,
We share tales of wonder, as friends often do.
In nature's embrace, where laughter is found,
We weave our own stories, both silly and sound.

www.ingramcontent.com/pod-product-compliance
Lightning Source LLC
Chambersburg PA
CBHW070333120526
44590CB00017B/2865